Trackers
Variety Fiction
Teacher's Guide

Contents

KATE RUTTLE
Series Editor

OXFORD
UNIVERSITY PRESS

OXFORD
UNIVERSITY PRESS

Great Clarendon Street, Oxford OX2 6DP

Oxford University Press is a department of the University of Oxford.
It furthers the University's objective of excellence in research,
scholarship, and education by publishing worldwide in

Oxford   New York
Auckland   Cape Town   Dar es Salaam   Hong Kong   Karachi
Kuala Lumpur   Madrid   Melbourne   Mexico City   Nairobi
New Delhi   Shanghai   Taipei   Toronto

With offices in

Argentina   Austria   Brazil   Chile   Czech Republic   France   Greece
Guatemala   Hungary   Italy   Japan   Poland   Portugal   Singapore
South Korea   Switzerland   Thailand   Turkey   Ukraine   Vietnam

Oxford is a registered trade mark of Oxford University Press
in the UK and in certain other countries

British Library Cataloguing in Publication Data

Data available

ISBN 978-0-19-8385493

3 5 7 9 10 8 6 4

Illustrations by Jane Bottomley and Tony Linsell

Typeset by Fakenham Photosetting, Fakenham, Norfolk

Printed in Great Britain by Ashford Colour Press.

Acknowledgements

The authors of the *Trackers* series would like to thank the many 'behind the scenes' people who have
worked so hard to make this project such fun. In particular we owe thanks to the talented and
industrious team at Oxford University Press whose enthusiasm and dedication to all aspects of the
project has been unwavering and infectious. We are also extremely grateful for the skill and hard
work of the freelance people we have been lucky enough to work with, in particular to Anne Priestley.

Trackers has been trialled in many different schools around England and we are grateful for all the
enthusiastic feedback from the teachers and children as well as those of our invaluable reviewers.
Thank you everybody for your comments. We have read and discussed them all and your feedback
has helped us to make the books even better!

Kate Ruttle

Introduction

The *Trackers* series of books is a carefully structured fiction and non-fiction reading resource for children aged 7+ who have a reading age of 5+. The books are particularly suitable for children who:

★ are finding reading a struggle,
★ are reluctant to read, or
★ are acquiring English as an additional language.

The two main aims of *Trackers* are:

★ to provide motivating 'must read' books with an interest age of 7+ and which matches the conceptual development of these children, while having a reading age of 5+;
★ to develop children's comprehension skills through generating an expectation that reading is concerned with 'getting meaning off the page', using a variety of strategies and cueing systems.

Trackers components and levels

Trackers level	National Curriculum level	Interest age	Pupil reading books	Teaching material
Starter Bear tracks	England & Wales – 1C Scotland – working towards level A N. Ireland – working within level 1	7+ years	6 non-fiction (16pp) 4 fiction (16pp) 2 variety fiction (16pp)	Teacher's Guide for Starter level Teacher's Guide for Trackers Variety Fiction (for all levels) Guided Reading Booklet for every title
1 Elephant tracks	England & Wales – 1B Scotland – working within level A N. Ireland – working towards level 2	7+ years	6 non-fiction (16pp) 4 fiction (16pp) 2 variety fiction (16pp)	Teacher's Guide for levels 1 and 2
2 Frog tracks	England & Wales – 1B/A Scotland – working within level A N. Ireland – working towards level 2	7+ years	6 non-fiction (16pp) 4 fiction (16pp) 2 variety fiction (16pp)	Guided Reading Booklet for every title
3 Giraffe tracks	England & Wales – 1A Scotland – working towards level B N. Ireland – working within level 2	8+ years	6 non-fiction (16pp) 4 fiction (16pp) 2 variety fiction (16pp)	Teacher's Guide for levels 3 and 4
4 Parrot tracks	England & Wales – 1A/2C Scotland – working towards level B N. Ireland – working within level 2	8+ years	6 non-fiction (24pp) 4 fiction (24pp) 2 variety fiction (24pp)	Guided Reading Booklet for every title
5 Tiger tracks	England & Wales – 2C Scotland – working within level B N. Ireland – working within level 2	9+ years	6 non-fiction (24pp) 4 fiction (24pp) 2 variety fiction (24pp)	Teacher's Guide for levels 5 and 6
6 Zebra tracks	England & Wales – 2B Scotland – working within level B N. Ireland – working within level 2	9+ years	6 non-fiction (24pp) 4 fiction (24pp) 2 variety fiction (24pp)	Guided Reading Booklet for every title

How do* Trackers *differ from books designed for younger children?

By the time children are 7+, they will have had previous experience of reading, albeit not always successful. This means that *Trackers* can make assumptions that children understand how reading 'works' (for example the eye-movement is from left to right across the page; book language has its own conventions; readers have different expectations of fiction and non-fiction books). *Trackers* books differ from books whose target audience is children aged 4+ in a number of key ways:

★ All the books look like books for older children; they are not printed in large font with very simple illustrations but have age appropriate illustrations and are printed in a variety of appropriately sized typefaces.

★ *Trackers* books are designed to grab the reader's attention and to make the children want to read and re-read them. Given that many children in the target audience have not found reading to be a rewarding experience, *Trackers* books work extra hard to provide that added incentive.

★ The design of each book is varied to suit the contents of the book. This is consistent with other books in the 7+ classroom.

★ The non-fiction books look like other non-fiction books available in school and class libraries. For instance, they make use of more sophisticated information presentation devices like simple charts, graphs and tables and the text is not consistently placed on all pages.

★ The non-fiction books include real, 'new' information which is age appropriate. Many non-fiction books for younger children won't add to older children's general knowledge – *Trackers* will!

★ The fiction story lines are more sophisticated than those used in the early stages of 'traditional' reading schemes and are aimed at the more mature humour and understanding of the slightly older child.

★ The books are longer than comparable books in traditional reading schemes and there is more text on the page. Since we are providing books for older children, the traditional eight-page 'small books for small hands' approach is unnecessary, as is the idea that there should only be one line of text on a page. If the text is accessible and interesting, older children can cope with two or three lines of text, even in the very earliest stages, and often need this quantity of text to give a good 'run in' so that comprehension strategies will work.

Are different* Trackers *titles aimed at children in particular year groups?

No. *Trackers* are aimed at any child aged between about 7 and 12 whose reading attainment matches the book. The reading profiles on pages 47 and 48 will give more guidance as to which *Trackers* level a child is best suited for, but readership is intended to be determined by reading ability, not chronological age.

Do* Trackers *support the National Literacy Strategy and the National Curriculum in England and Wales?

Yes. Although none of the books is specifically linked to particular reading objectives (in order that they are not seen to be directed at any particular age group) the texts are carefully written to be rich enough in both language and content for age-appropriate discussions and investigations. The Key Stage 2 and 3 objectives in the NLS (National Literacy Strategy) have been borne in mind both in the texts and in the Guided Reading Booklets which accompany each text.

The non-fiction text types chosen for *Trackers* are those specified most commonly in the *NLS Framework* and the topics are all relevant to the National Curriculum and to the QCA programmes of study.

Do* Trackers *support the Education 5–14 guidelines in Scotland and the National Curriculum in Northern Ireland?

Yes. All the *Trackers* titles have been checked by experts in Scotland and do support the guidelines, both in literacy and across the wider curriculum. Again, no specific references and objectives are shown, but expected learning outcomes are made explicit.

Do* Trackers *help to accelerate reading ability?

Yes, in two main ways:

★ *By promoting age-appropriate reading skills*
Children aged 7+ who struggle with reading tend to experience difficulty across the curriculum because information and resources are increasingly delivered through the written word. Many children who find reading difficult are otherwise capable of accessing an

age-appropriate curriculum and these children need to develop 'book awareness' understanding (e.g. how non-fiction books are organised; how authors create characters and settings) in order that they can track the progress made by their peers.

★ *By challenging children to try to read slightly more complex language*

All **Trackers** books have two levels of text: the main text which is very structured (see pages 7–8) and additional 'secondary' text which is slightly more challenging. Experience shows that most of the children who could read the main text in a book were eager to attempt the more challenging secondary text and they were often successful.

What is the difference between 'main text' and 'secondary text'?

Main text The main text in each book is carefully structured to promote gradual, secure progression through the development of different skills and strategies for reading (see page 7). In the non-fiction books, this text is always clearly marked by some design device which is identified on the inside front cover of each book. If children only read the main text in any book, the book will make complete sense and be a satisfying read.

The main text is intended to be at the child's instructional level (i.e. they can read about 90–95% independently and accurately). This is the text children should work at independently in guided reading sessions.

The main text is used to calculate the word count, phonic focus and high frequency words for each book.

Secondary text In many of the books there is additional text whose purpose varies depending on the text type or genre. The secondary text is usually at the level above the main text, so when the children move to the next level of **Trackers** they will be well prepared for its challenges.

This secondary text has three main functions:
★ to offer an additional level of challenge which encourages children to try to stretch their reading abilities within a secure and motivating context;
★ to give additional information which increases the readership of the book and the understanding and enjoyment of each reader;
★ to provide age-appropriate book features which can be mediated by an adult to help to develop the children's age-appropriate reading behaviours and understanding.

In the non-fiction, some features are consistently counted as secondary text in all text types. These include:
★ *all the organisational features of the books* (contents page, index, headings, glossaries, blurb). It is expected that these features will primarily be used in the context of an adult teaching the children to use these features efficiently and correctly to find information. Most of the words used for headings etc. are 'content' words which are easily read in the context of the pictures and the on-going text, but which are not expected to be read in isolation. Since they are read with an adult, glossaries and indexes include words from the secondary text throughout the book.
★ *The 'look back' section.* Most of the non-fiction books include a 'look back' section which encourages children to revisit the book to find specific information. The index is printed on the same double-page spread as the look back section in order that the children can be taught to make use of the index to find answers to the questions. Again, it is anticipated that this activity will be mediated by an adult, so the 'look back' section is secondary text.

Text types and genres

Trackers includes books from a range of text types and genres because they present different reading challenges and offer opportunities for teaching a variety of reading strategies (including, for instance: a range of purposes for reading, a variety of comprehension strategies and different strategies for decoding print).

Trackers non-fiction books are written by Sarah Fleming using a variety of non-fiction text types and address a wide range of subjects, many of which can be used across the curriculum. These books encourage reading for meaning, understanding and new information. The *Trackers* fiction books (Space School Stories) are all written by Paul Shipton and feature the same set of characters in their fantasy setting on the planet Zap. The books encourage confidence in reading for meaning and enjoyment.

The *Trackers* Variety Fiction books are written by a variety of authors so that children can experience different authorial voices. This is a new challenge because when children first open a book they can bring little prior knowledge to bear on the characters, the settings, and the likelihood of a humorous or suspense story. It is important for children to read books written by different authors so that they learn how to recognise and use all the clues about a book which are available from the cover, the blurb, the illustration style, and the content and style of writing of the first few pages. Reading a wide range of authors and genres also enables them to develop opinions about books; even children who struggle with reading need to develop the confidence to talk about their own responses to a book, a style or an author. *Trackers* Variety Fiction helps children not just to learn to read but to become readers.

There are 14 *Trackers* Variety Fiction books, all of which are written by established children's authors:

Level	Title	Author	Genre
Starter Bear tracks	*Stop That Ball*	Alan MacDonald	Familiar settings (football)
Starter Bear tracks	*Up to You, Sam*	Chris Powling	Familiar settings (pets)
1 Elephant tracks	*Billy the Hero*	Alan Brown	Familiar settings (humour)
1 Elephant tracks	*A Cat's Tail*	Stephen Elboz	Familiar settings (family)
2 Frog tracks	*A Very Cross Country*	Steve Barlow and Steve Skidmore	Familiar settings (PE – school)
2 Frog tracks	*Cool!*	Susan Gates	Familiar settings (talents)
3 Giraffe tracks	*Rover*	Jon Blake	Fantasy (pets)
3 Giraffe tracks	*Jake's Alien*	Jan Mark	Fantasy (aliens)
4 Parrot tracks	*Air Raid*	Jill Atkins	Historical (WW2)
4 Parrot tracks	*The Worst Ghost of All*	Helena Pielichaty	Fantasy (ghosts)
5 Tiger tracks	*Super Socks*	Douglas Hill	Fantasy (football)
5 Tiger tracks	*The Blue Bog Baby*	Helena Pielichaty	Fantasy (humour)
6 Zebra tracks	*The Hole*	Robert Swindells	Adventure/historical (school)
6 Zebra tracks	*Avalanche*	Alan Gibbons	Adventure (mountain walking)

Structure

The development of skills through *Trackers* is carefully structured to ensure that children make appropriate progress while existing skills are consolidated and made secure. In order to give opportunities for adequate reinforcement, there is a mixture of fiction and non-fiction books, and seven levels of books to span the reading ages from approximately 5:6 to 7:6.

The level descriptions in the Book Bands reference book have been used to give guidance as to text features which are appropriate at each level, but since *Trackers* is aimed at an older target readership, some of the Book Bands level descriptors are inappropriate (for example, we have a greater amount of text on a page; we have more pages in a book; we have more

complex story lines). We have, however, structured the degree of support given to the reader through features such as:

★ consistency of sentence structure and how closely sentence structure reflects spoken language;
★ predictability of story line;
★ relationship between text and pictures;
★ phonic skills necessary to decode phonically regular words;
★ percentage of high frequency, or phonically regular, words.

The following table shows the structured progression within *Trackers* of some of these skills and strategies.

Trackers level	Word count (see also text type descriptions)	Number of pages	Phonic focus	High frequency words
Starter	60–190	16	CVC words*	35
Level 1	75–400	16	Initial and final consonant blends	+25
Level 2	150–475	16	Initial and final consonant blends	+15
Level 3	300–510	16	Introducing common long vowel phonemes	+20
Level 4	500–720	24	Consolidating common long vowel phonemes	+30
Level 5	620–920	24	Introducing other long vowel phonemes	+50
Level 6	690–970	24	Consolidating other long vowel phonemes	+50

* Note that CVC words are defined as being words made up of three phonemes: consonant, short vowel phoneme, consonant. Although most CVC words are written with three letters, e.g. *cut, big, fed*, some consonant phonemes are represented by two letters, so words such as *ship, this, wish* are included as CVC words.

★ *Word count and number of pages* The rise in word count and page numbers reflects the expectation that reading stamina and proficiency are developing. The variations of word count within a level are appropriate to the different text types.
★ *Phonic focus* This progression of phonic skills is consistent with that recommended in DfES phonics programmes. The 'phonic focus' does not imply that the books exclusively use words with these letter patterns, but that there is a preponderance of such words where possible.

This is particularly apparent in the fiction books.
★ *High frequency words* These are words which are used frequently across all the books in a level.

Other, less measurable, ways in which *Trackers* books are structured are:
★ *Content* The earlier books, both fiction and non-fiction, have cognitively less demanding content than the later books. As the children read through the levels they will encounter increasingly demanding ideas.

* *'Word attack' strategies* In the Guided Reading Booklets for the first levels, fairly simple strategies are suggested which build on familiar strategies children have been developing since they began reading (e.g. sounding out and sounding out by syllable). During level 3, more 'meaning based' strategies are introduced and children are also asked to segment words into familiar letter patterns as they meet more long vowel sounds.
* *Page design* Although designers always design books individually, there are fewer constraints in the higher levels. This means, for example, that there are some pages which have a lot more text on them than others. This is consistent with other age-appropriate books children will meet in the classroom. The text will, of course, still be very structured, but the books will increasingly look like other books in the class library.
* *Comprehension focus* Different kinds of comprehension are the focus of different questions posed in the Guided Reading Booklets. 'Retrieval of detail' questions are suggested to help children to focus on what they have actually read in the book; 'simple inference' questions encourage children to reflect on what they have read and to draw their own conclusions; and 'personal response' questions ask children to give their opinions and to relate what they have read to their own experiences. As children progress through *Trackers*, more searching questions are suggested which require children to use more inferential and deductive comprehension. These require a greater understanding of the text and challenge children to think harder about what they have read.

Reading *Trackers* Variety Fiction

In recognition of the fact that the authors and the stories are unfamiliar to the children, we recommend that you always prepare the children before they begin to read the Variety Fiction books for themselves. There are different approaches to 'preparing' the children which can support readers at different stages:
* *Reading aloud* Simply read all the text aloud to the child. Try to avoid commenting on the events in the story or the pictures until you have finished reading because children can find it hard to distinguish which of the words are in the text and which are yours. Reading a book aloud is very supportive because it gives children:
  * the vocabulary and rhythms of the author's language;
  * a clear understanding of the characters, events and shape of the story;
  * a model of good reading, with appropriate intonation.
* *Pre-reading* Skim read the book while the child watches and listens. As you skim read, point out repeated words and phrases, and words you think the child might find tricky, including names; read the occasional sentence aloud to demonstrate the rhythm of the language; tell the child the outline of the story using pictures as well as words and phrases. Reading in this way is less supportive than reading aloud, but it is useful because it gives children:
  * the confidence to tackle tricky words and names;
  * some idea about the style of language in the book;
  * an understanding of the characters, events and the broad shape of the story.
* *Silent reading* Give children time to read the book to themselves and to look at the pictures before they try to read it out loud. While they read to themselves, let them ask you for help with any tricky words they encounter. Once children have had time to look at the book, they can read it aloud to you. This approach gives children:
  * greater independence and potentially more ownership of the book, because they have only heard it read in their own voice;
  * the opportunity to identify tricky words before they read aloud, but also the pressure of having to work out some of the words while reading silently;
  * the chance to find out what they can from the text and pictures before they read to you, so they have some idea of the story events, characters and setting.

If children are new to reading *Trackers* Variety Fiction books, and are at the lower levels, you will probably want to read the story aloud before the children attempt it. As they grow more confident, you can reduce the support you offer in the preparation stages.

Using *Trackers* in the classroom

Trackers books are intended to be used for three purposes:
1. for children to browse through, enjoy and share with their friends and family;
2. for guided reading, supported by either a teacher or a teaching assistant;
3. for children to return to for the exciting and rewarding experience of re-reading a favourite book.

Using *Trackers* for guided reading

To support you in using *Trackers* for guided reading, each *Trackers* book is accompanied by:
★ pages in this Teacher's Guide that give you all the information you need about each book, including the summary of the book, lists of high frequency and content words, phonic focus and information about the photocopy master (PCM) worksheets;
★ two PCMs for each book. For all the books, the first PCM addresses word level skills that help to develop reading fluency and accuracy. The second PCM focuses on reading comprehension or scaffolds a writing task based on the book.
★ a Guided Reading Booklet.

Guided Reading Booklet
The Guided Reading Booklet can be used by teaching assistants or parent helpers working with a group, pairs or individual pupils. It includes a format for organising guided reading sessions and suggests ways to introduce each book so that the children are more likely to achieve success. There are also discussion points for a final session in which the children consider what they have achieved. This final section includes comprehension questions that develop SATs-type comprehension skills, focusing on 'retrieval of detail', 'simple inference' and 'personal response'.

In addition, the Guided Reading Booklet gives page by page suggestions, including:
★ discussion points to ensure that children understand the progression of the text;
★ ways of introducing and exploring 'tricky' words that are appropriate to the reading strategies being developed.

Home/school links using *Trackers*

Children will enjoy reading *Trackers* so much that they will be keen to take them home to re-read with parents and carers. Depending on your school policy, you may be happy to send the books home, or you may prefer to keep sets intact in school. Either way, the PCMs for each book can make good homework activities. For this reason, at least one of the PCMs for each book can be completed without direct reference to the *Trackers* book (although children will need to have read the *Trackers* book in order to understand the activity).

Which level of *Trackers* should a child be reading?

As you become more familiar with *Trackers*, you will gain a better understanding of how it fits with other reading resources you use, and which children will read most happily at which levels. The following chart may be helpful:

Trackers level	Associated Book Band level	Approximate National Curriculum level	Scottish 5–14 level	NI Curriculum level
Starter Bear tracks	Yellow	1C	Working within level A	Working within level 1
1 Elephant tracks	Blue	1B	Working within level A	Working towards level 2
2 Frog tracks	Green	1B/A	Working within level A	Working towards level 2
3 Giraffe tracks	Orange	1A	Working towards level B	Working within level 2
4 Parrot tracks	Turquoise	1A/2C	Working towards level B	Working within level 2
5 Tiger tracks	Purple	2C	Working within level B	Working within level 2
6 Zebra tracks	Gold	2B	Working within level B	Working within level 2

Using the *Trackers* Reading Profile

Photocopy the appropriate Reading Profile from page 47 or page 48 and use it as you do a detailed assessment of children's reading skills and strategies, and their knowledge about reading. The statements summarise the skills needed to read the particular level. The statements at each level are not mutually exclusive and it is unlikely that any one of the profiles will exactly match each child. You can use the profile to do a 'best fit' assessment to make initial decisions before trying out *Trackers* at that level.

* If a child cannot read unknown CVC (consonant–vowel–consonant) words and can't track a text from left to right across a page, then *Trackers* is probably too challenging.
* If you can tick some, but not all of the *Bear tracks* statements, then the child is probably ready to read **Bear tracks**.
* If you can tick all the *Bear tracks* and some of the *Elephant tracks* statements, then the child is probably ready to begin reading **Elephant tracks**, and so on for the succeeding levels.

Trackers Variety Fiction and the literacy lesson

Most of the major fiction genres which children commonly read at Primary School are represented in *Trackers* Variety Fiction. If you are studying a particular genre in your literacy lessons, allow a group of children to do a parallel study using one of the Variety Fiction books. These books are written using all the expected text features of the genre and the stories are rich enough to be revisited for different purposes. Although children may struggle with reading, many of them are capable of age-appropriate responses to a text and *Trackers* can be used to develop these skills.

Comprehension

The key focus of all *Trackers* books is on reading for meaning and the additional focus of Variety Fiction is on developing a personal response to a text. In order for children to really understand a text, they need to be prepared to revisit the text, asking different question on each visit. To begin with the questions can be of the simple *who, what, where, when* type, for example:

* *Who* are the main characters?

* *What* happened in the story?
* *Where* were the characters?
* *When* did the main event happen?

These questions can be answered using literal comprehension and children can find words and phrases in the text to answer them.

On a following visit to the text, children can begin to consider trickier *why* and *how* questions like:

* *Why* did this happen?
* *How* did the character feel? How do I know?

Through these questions, the reader starts comparing the characters to him- or herself and thus giving motives for their actions. In order to answer questions like these, the reader has to used inference and deduction to find the information that the author has hinted at, but not written.

Considering setting and character

In all of the *Trackers* Variety Fiction books, the authors have told the story using a comparatively small number of words; they haven't had much space for description. Encourage children to think about the characters and setting and to consider *how* they know what they know. Some of the information is in the pictures, but the skilled authors also give a lot of information in the text.

Encourage children to look at:

* *Powerful verbs* These can tell us about how characters are feeling and reacting as well as how they do things.
* *Dialogue* We learn a lot about characters by how they speak.
* *Reactions* The way that characters react to people and events in books tells us a lot about them.
* *Adjectives and adverbs* Often, one well chosen adjective or adverb can create a powerful setting.
* *Characters' names and place names* We can learn a lot about the author's view of their characters by considering their names.

Once children are aware of the way in which authors can create characters and settings in a small number of words, encourage them to use some of these stories as models for their own writing.

Authorial voice

Even after they have decided what the story is about, authors still have to make choices when they are writing. Some of the choices they make include:

★ *The choice of person who is telling the story* Will the narrator be a character so the story becomes told in the first person? – *I stared at him.* Or will the narrator be an onlooker, telling the story in the third person? – *She stared at him.*

★ *The tense* Stories are usually told in the past tense, but sometimes they are more persuasive if told in the present tense.

★ *The tone* Is the story going to be told in a light-hearted, funny style, or a heavy, serious style? The same story can be told in quite different styles, with different effects on the reader.

★ *The language* Will the story rhyme? Will there be patterned language, where a word or phrase is repeated at different points in the story? Will the author use mostly long sentences or short ones? Will the author try to match sentence length to whatever is happening, e.g. if someone is thinking while they are running, will the sentences be short and breathless, or if they are tired, will the sentences peter out without being finished?

As children become readers, they can learn to be aware of the skill and craft of the author. Questions like those above are at the heart of literacy teaching for children aged 7+ and can be considered using the *Trackers* Variety Fiction books.

Other books by *Trackers Variety Fiction* authors

Cold Heart of Summer by Alan Gibbons (Barrington Stoke);
Room 13 by Robert Swindells (Corgi Children's Books);
Snow Maze by Jan Mark (Sprinters – Walker Books);
Yummy Scrummy by Alan MacDonald (OUP).

Speaking and listening

Some of the children who struggle with reading, particularly for whom English is an additional or foreign language, are likely to find speaking and listening challenging. This is often because they feel inadequate when faced by their more articulate peers and they don't think that they have a valid contribution to make to a discussion. Encouraging such children to develop their speaking and listening skills is crucial both for their self-esteem and to promote their own intellectual development.

Trackers supports speaking and listening development in a number of key ways:

★ *Through group discussion* Issues arising from the books can be developed in group discussion. Through these discussions with equals, children can develop age-appropriate responses to, and expectations of, the stories. Many of the stories are based around issues which can enrich PHSE enquiries and promote empathy with characters.

★ *Through the exciting content and design* **Trackers** books are designed to be poured over and discussed by pairs of children.

★ *Through the Guided Reading Booklets* Each *Trackers* book has a Guided Reading Booklet to accompany it which is full of opportunities to develop ideas and concepts through speaking and listening.

Reading and writing

Many children who experience difficulties with reading also find writing challenging. Although *Trackers* is primarily a reading resource, it also promotes writing development:

★ *By providing good models of text* Children find it difficult to write different kinds of texts if they are not familiar with the basic conventions and language use of the text type. By providing a wide range of well written texts – albeit using comparatively simple language structures – *Trackers* offers good models on which children can base their own writing.

★ *By scaffolding planning activities* Many of the photocopy master (PCM) worksheets support children in thinking about the structure and language of texts. Activities include sequencing events in a story, summarising stories, considering how characters are reacting to an event in the story. The activities have a dual purpose: to help children to develop key skills for planning and writing while reinforcing skills for reading for different purposes.

Trackers Variety Fiction Starter level: Bear tracks

> **Author:** Alan MacDonald
> **Illustrator:** Doffy Wier

Stop That Ball

At the football match, Jess's job is to get the ball when it is kicked off the pitch. But the ball goes right out of the ground and Jess has to find it.

Total number of words: 156   Number of different words: 62

10 useful high frequency words
a, but, dog, got, it, ran, she, the, to, was

'Tricky' words
after, asked, began, coach, dropped, fetch, first, football, goal, ground, jumped, looked, match, out, over, picked, puddle, saw, school, signed, stopped, team, workman

Words with CVC
back, but, dog, get, got, Jess, job, let, ran, then, wet

PCM 1 (p.13) hearing 'b' anywhere in a word
★ Identify all the pictures together.
★ Children then say the words to themselves and decide whether or not each contains a 'b'. If it does, they should tick the 'yes' box.

PCM 2 (p.14) finding information
★ Children cut out the pictures and sequence them.
★ Ask pairs of children to retell the story to each other, using the picture sequence.

> **Author:** Chris Powling
> **Illustrator:** Jane Bottomley

Up to You, Sam

Mum and Dad said that Sam could have a pet, any pet. Sam wanted a gorilla, so they went to the shops to look for one.

Total number of words: 185   Number of different words: 55

10 useful high frequency words
Dad, dog, can, Mum, they, to, up, we, went, you

'Tricky' words
after, come, gorilla, I'd, I'll, it's, let's, last, looked, more, one, sorry, was

Words with CVC
big, but, can, cat, Dad, did, dog, fed, get, let, mad, Mum, Sam, shop, that, then, this

PCM 1 (p.15) recognising medial vowels
★ Talk about the range of choices to complete each of the words before the children start to work. For example, two of the letter combinations can use all five vowels (p–t, b–g).
★ Once they have made the words, they can look for them in the book. Some of the words they have made will not be in the book. They should only record those that are.

PCM 2 (p.16) finding information
★ Children should cut out the speech bubbles, then read the text on the pages to find out what Sam said.
★ Point out that, in the book, the words that Sam said are those inside the speech marks.

Hearing b

Is there a **b** in the word?

Yes	No

Yes	No

Yes	No

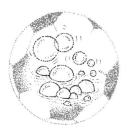

Yes	No

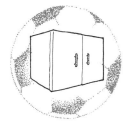

Yes	No

Yes	No

Yes	No

Yes	No

Yes	No

Yes	No

Yes	No

Draw something
with **b** in it.

Focus: hearing 'b' anywhere in a word

Where did the ball go?

Cut out the pictures to show the order.

Draw something else that happened to the ball.

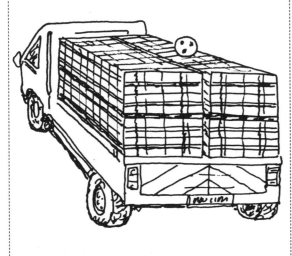

Focus: finding information

Finish the word

Choose a vowel to finish each word.
Make as many words as you can.

p_t   g_t

M_m   b_g

d_g   m_d

D_d   c_t

b_t   sh_p

c_n

Which of these words can you see on:

page 5? _____

page 6? _____

pages 10 and 11? _____

pages 12 and 13? _____

Write the words.

What did Sam say?

What did Sam say? Stick each speech bubble on the correct picture.

page 3

page 6

a friend for life!

page 12

Write what Sam said in the speech bubble.

...iend ...r life!

page 14

Cut out the speech bubbles.

OK, I'd like a gorilla.

OK, I'll have a cat or a dog.

But it's up to me.

Focus: finding information

Trackers Variety Fiction level 1: Elephant tracks

> **Author:** Alan Brown
> **Illustrator:** Chris Moulds

Billy the Hero

Billy's Mum is having a baby. Billy wants to help but he can't quite remember what Mum wants him to do because he didn't listen.

Total number of words: 204   Number of different words: 85

10 useful high frequency words
did, for, he, it, like, not, said, she, to, what

'Tricky' words
baby, broke, cook, grass, hero, hospital, iron, listen, loved, now, phone, shirts, sister, take, wanted, wash, window

Words with consonant blends
dishes, help, grass, list, lunch, mend, socks, thanks, went

PCM 1 (p.18) finding rhyming words
★ Read the words together.
★ Children draw lines to join the pairs of words that rhyme. Talk about the spelling patterns in the words.

PCM 2 (p.19) finding information
★ Read the things that Mum wanted to do. Then ask children to find what Billy did instead each time. They should write and draw the answer.

> **Author:** Stephen Elboz
> **Illustrator:** Trevor Dinton

A Cat's Tail

Gran has an ugly china cat without a tail. She takes it to a TV show to see what they think of it but it smashes.

Total number of words: 246   Number of different words: 82

10 useful high frequency words
at, cat, in, look, one, said, she, this, what, with

'Tricky' words
all, china, floor, found, girl, gold, happy, house, little, old, people, saw, show, table, tail, treasure, under

Words with consonant blends
crash, grabbed, Gran, gold, hand, just, next, old, things, went

PCM 1 (p.20) identifying final sounds in words
★ Discuss what the words should be.
★ Children should try to complete the words independently before finding them in the book.

PCM 2 (p.21) comprehension
★ Read the sentences together.
★ Discuss the meaning of 'true' and 'false' and agree the answers to the first few statements.

Find the rhyme

Join the pairs of rhyming words.

telly

dish

cat

sock

Mum

thumb

lock

smelly

cook

Draw something that
rhymes with cook.

fish

mat

18

Focus: finding rhyming words

What did Billy do wrong?

Where you see , draw or write what Billy did.

What Mum wanted...	What Billy did...

Feed the cat.	Wash the cat.

Wash the dishes.	
Iron the shirts.	

Focus: finding information

What's that sound?

Take letters from the cat's tail and use them to finish the words.

Gra_   ca_   sho_

ol_   ma_   nex_

han_   bi_   bo_

gol_   happ_   tai_

Ring the words you can find in the book and write the page number beside each word.

Focus: identifying final sounds in words

True or false?

Read the sentences. Are they true or false?

	True	False
Gran likes TV.	✓	
Gran is old.		
Gran's cat was hidden in the attic.		
Gran's cat was made of glass.		
Gran took a dish to the show.		
The man liked Gran's cat.		
Gran hit the table.		
There was a box in the cat.		
The map said look under the floor.		
There was gold in the box.		

Write two more true sentences about the story.

_____

_____

_____

_____

_____

Focus: comprehension

Trackers Variety Fiction level 2: Frog tracks

> **Author:** Steve Barlow and Steve Skidmore
> **Illustrator:** Andy Hammond

A Very Cross Country

Ben and Tim hate cross country running, especially when it's raining. They see a short cut across a field. But there's a bull in the field.

Total number of words: 275   Number of different words: 110

10 useful high frequency words
be, cross, find, first, for, go, have, that, they, very

'Tricky' words
across, ahead, always, country, cow, didn't, fair, field, find, first, hate, how, last, lives, near, now, out, their, want, way, we'll, which, why

Words with consonant blends
back, bull, class, cross, fast, jumped, just, last, past, plan, rest, smell, step, stop, think, want

PCM 1 (p.23) identifying real words
★ Read all the words in each line to the children, asking them to raise their hands when they hear a real word.
★ The children should then hunt for the real word on each line to make a path across the field.

PCM 2 (p.24) comprehension
★ Read the sentence beginnings and endings together before the children complete the activity.

> **Author:** Susan Gates
> **Illustrator:** Martin Impey

Cool!

"No more painting," said Jo's Mum. "It gets you into trouble." So Jo tries to find something else to do.

Total number of words: 223   Number of different words: 83

10 useful high frequency words
but, did, didn't, had, he, liked, many, next, saw, they

'Tricky' words
boy, coat, even, many, now, our, painted, painting, park, skate, skateboard, stay, trouble, walls

Words with consonant blends
best, crept, felt, jump, just, next, thanks, things, went

PCM 1 (p.25) making regular past tense forms
★ Do the work orally first, checking that children understand which words -ed or -d can be added to, and why.
★ Discuss the distribution of -ed and -d.

PCM 2 (p.26) empathising with a character
★ Talk about how Jo might have felt each time, and why.
★ Children should cut out the faces and complete the activity independently.

Which words are real?

Some of the words are real. Some are not.
Make a safe path across the field by joining the real words.

closs	cross	cros

run	rin	rup	ret	rop

wut	wat	wet	wup	wep

cless	cluss	closs	class	cliss

sec	sic	sak	sik	seck	sick

pran	plon	plan	plen	plin	plun

gate	gute	gite	gete	gaet

boll	bal	bel	bull	bul	bil

Focus: identifying real words

Finish the sentences

Find the correct ending for each sentence. Write them in the spaces.

Tim and Ben didn't like cross country because	
Ben had to stop because	
They went across a field because	
They ran very fast across the field because	
They fell into a cow pat because	Finish the sentence yourself.

Choose from these endings:

... he felt sick.

... they wanted to be first.

... the bull ran fast.

... they were no good at running.

Focus: comprehension

Can you add -ed?

Ring all the words you can add **-ed** or **-d** to.
Write the **-ed** word on the skateboard.

paint

like

got

felt

call

go

run

skate

jump

said

stay

fell

Write words you can add **-d** or **-ed** to on these skateboards.

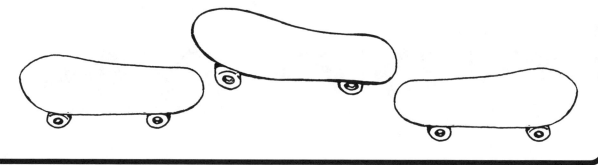

Focus: making regular past tense forms

25

How did Jo feel when ...?

Cut out the picture of Jo that shows how she felt when ...

Stick the picture that shows how Jo felt here.

... she was painting.	
... Mum said "No painting!"	
... she saw the kids skate.	
... she fell off the skateboard.	
... the kids looked at her and she crept away.	
Write something that made Jo feel happy at the end of the story.	

Cut out these pictures and stick them in the right place.

Focus: empathising with a character

Trackers Variety Fiction level 3: Giraffe tracks

Author: Jon Blake
Illustrator: Jane Bottomley

Rover

Josh went to the pet shop to buy a dog, and ended up with Rover – a giant pet with eight hairy legs and eight eyes.

Total number of words: 211   Number of different words: 94

10 useful high frequency words
as, big, children, eat, for, have, him, his, saw, want

'Tricky' words
around, corner, enormous, eyes, fetch, gone, great, hugged, hungry, morning, over, spider, tickle, trained

Useful long vowel phonemes
'ai': *day, great, race, stay, train*
'ee': *he, sleep, three*
'oa': *home, no, only, over, roll, Rover, woke*

PCM 1 (p.28) finding words with the long vowel phoneme 'ai'
★ Read the words at the bottom of the sheet to the children, asking children to raise their hands when they hear a word with long vowel phoneme.

★ The children should then work independently to complete the activity.
PCM 2 (p.29) finding information
★ Children may need to look through the book to answer these questions.

Author: Jan Mark
Illustrator: Mike Phillips

Jake's Alien

Jake wakes up one morning to find an alien on his bed. The alien wants to be taken to Jake's leader, so Jake takes him to his teacher.

Total number of words: 330   Number of different words: 109

10 useful high frequency words
be, has, know, next, school, small, take, teacher, very, what

'Tricky' words
alien, corner, dream, globe, gone, know, leader, morning, over, person, slime, space, Spalien, teacher, want, world, you're

Useful long vowel phonemes
'ai': *alien, came, Jake, name, space, Spalien, take, taken*
'ee': *be, dream, green, he, leader, me, please, sleep, teacher*
'oa': *globe, glow, go, know, woke*

PCM 1 (p.30) identifying words with the split digraph 'e'
★ Work out what the words should be together.
★ Check that the children understand when the 'e' is required (for these words, when there is a long vowel in the word).

PCM 2 (p.31) finding information
★ Ask children to think about what happened next in each case before they complete the activity. They may need to refer to the book.

Catching words

In the boxes, write words with the same long vowel phoneme as in **c<u>a</u>me**.

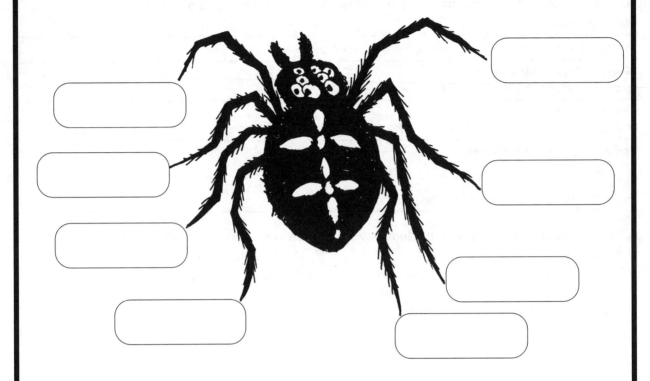

Choose from these words:

tame	trained	bead	Josh
rat	race	like	come
game	rain	woke	cake
Rover	tail	bug	grape

Find four more words with the <u>same</u> long vowel phoneme.

_____ _____ _____ _____

Focus: finding words with the long vowel phoneme 'ai'

Did he do it?

Which of these actions did Rover do?
Cross out the things he didn't do.

look at Josh with 8 big eyes

beg

jump up

fetch a stick

roll over

climb a tree

Draw and write two more things Rover <u>did</u> do.

-e or not -e?

Spalien has put slime at the end of all the words. Should there be an -e or not?
Write -e on the slime if there should be an -e.

alien

Jak

slim

spac

sleep

pleas

glob

lik

cam

dream

wok

tak

teacher

Write three more words that end with -e.

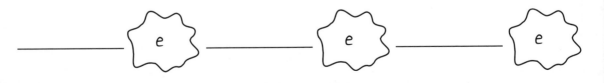

_____ e _____ e _____ e

Focus: identifying words with the split digraph 'e'

What happened next?

Draw and write a sentence to show what happened after ...

Jake woke up and saw an alien.

The alien said, "Then take me to your teacher."

Jake put Spalien on the shelf next to the globe.

Focus: finding information

Trackers Variety Fiction level 4: Parrot tracks

> **Author:** Jill Atkins
> **Illustrator:** Kathryn Baker

Air Raid

Peter and his family are safe in the air-raid shelter when the bomb falls. But the house next door is hit and Mr Smith is trapped. Only Peter can get him out.

Total number of words: 530   Number of different words: 230

10 useful high frequency words
after, again, all, away, by, can't, down, help, into, too

'Tricky' words
afraid, ambulance, bombs, bravely, clear, climbed, closer, could, dangerous, door, downstairs, explosion, kitchen, scared, siren, someone, whispered, whistling

Useful long vowel phonemes
'ai': *afraid, brave, came, day, faint, hated, made, pale, planes, raid, shaking, stayed, wailing, waited, way*
'ee': *he, indeed, leaf, me, need, screaming, see, squeezed, three*
'ie': *alive, climbed, cried, dived, light, night, pile, right, siren, time, try, wider, while*

PCM 1 (p.33) counting syllables
★ Check that children understand the idea of 'syllables'. Practise counting the syllables in their names and things around the room.
★ Read the words to the children while they count the syllables. They can then complete the activity independently.

PCM 2 (p.34) sequencing events
★ Children should cut out the dominoes. Read the information on each domino together before the children try to assemble the whole story.

> **Author:** Helena Pielichaty
> **Illustrator:** Vincent Viglo

The Worst Ghost of All

Mr Spit can't sell High House because it is full of ghosts. At last, one day, Lord C Threw says that he wants to buy it.

Total number of words: 436   Number of different words: 146

10 useful high frequency words
ago, all, asks, because, long, says, some, there, until, your

'Tricky' words
buy, death, died, dining, everyone, eyes, ghost, gone, haunted, high, kitchen, nasty, people, scary, threw, voice, worst

Useful long vowel phonemes
'ai': *day, hate, name, say, they*
'ee': *creepy, deep, he, me, scream, see, sleep, teeth, we*
'oa': *cold, don't, ghosts, goes, know, sold*

PCM 1 (p.35) silent letters
★ Read the words together.
★ Discuss the meaning of a 'silent' letter and work together to place the first few words.

PCM 2 (p.36) finding information
★ Read the sentence beginnings together and let the children use the book to find the sentence endings.

Counting syllables

Read the words. Count how many syllables there are in each. Write the words in the correct shelter.

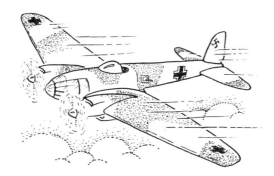

siren	~~Peter~~	~~Mum~~	Janet	darkness
way	little	night	jolt	kitchen
clicked	plane	cold	dark	afraid

Peter

2 syllables

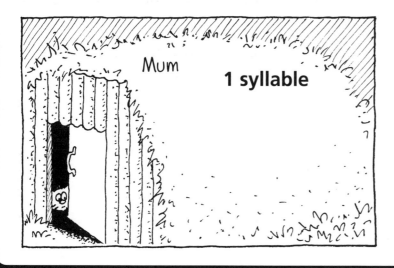

Mum

1 syllable

Find two more words in the book to write in each shelter.

What happened next?

Cut out the dominoes. Arrange them in a line to retell the story.

Start here.

The air raid siren went off.	Peter got out of bed and	they sat on the camp beds.	They heard the drone of a plane, then

there was an explosion. It was close.	The planes went away, then	Peter led the way to the shelter.	In the shelter, Mum lit candles and

went to get Janet.	Mum checked the black-out, then	the siren sounded the all-clear.	Outside, someone was screaming, so

Write what happened next.

there was a whistling sound.	The bombs fell. Just then	

Focus: sequencing events

Is it silent?

If the underlined letter is silent, write the word next to High House. If not, write the word next to the other house.

_____

_____

_____

_____

_____

ghost

spit

cold

throb

write

scream

knee   drop

scissors   crack

_____ _____

school

_____ _____

bedroom

_____ _____

_____ _____

went   what

_____

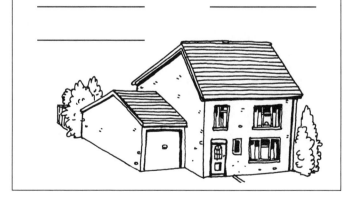

damp

Find three more words with silent letters.

_____ _____ _____

What do they do to you?

Finish the sentences.

Thin Jim screams at you until _____ 	Bossy Flossie screams at you until _____ 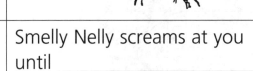
Scary Mary screams at you until _____ 	Smelly Nelly screams at you until _____ 
Draw your own ghost and write what happens when it screams at you.	Nasty Ned screams at you until _____ 
	Lord C Threw will scare you to death! 

Focus: finding information

Trackers Variety Fiction level 5: Tiger tracks

> **Author:** Douglas Hill
> **Illustrator:** Chris Fisher

Super Socks

When he wears Gran's socks, Rob is good at football. Why?

Total number of words: 632   Number of different words: 253

10 useful high frequency words
after, again, better, everyone, football, other, over, took, wear, when

'Tricky' words
anymore, anyone, aren't, captain, colours, different, everyone, fierce, goalkeeper, huge, idea, knew, knitting, laugh, new, noticed, often, orange, purple, scary, straight, they're, thought, towards, tremendous, watched, wild, you'll, you're

Useful long vowel phonemes
'ar': *after, are, far, fast, hard, hardly, last, laugh, past, scarves, star, start*
'ue': *boot, do, flew, grew, huge, knew, new, school, super, too, you*
'ie': *bright, light, might, silence, smiled, smiling, stripes, tried, wild*

PCM 1 (p.38) different spelling, same pronunciation
★ Remind children that the same sound can be represented by different spelling patterns.
★ Read the words on the sheet aloud before the children begin the activity.

PCM 2 (p.39) developing characterisation
★ Ask the children what they think Rob is feeling in each episode. Ask them to explain their responses.

> **Author:** Helena Pielichaty
> **Illustrator:** Sholto Walker

The Blue Bog Baby

Sid, Kitty and Amit can't possibly carry on with their building because Betty is giving birth to her Blue Bog Baby.

Total number of words: 732   Number of different words: 222

10 useful high frequency words
after, angry, began, blue, comes, does, everything, near, over, page

'Tricky' words
any, built, clipboard, crossword, does, explained, frowned, hearts, huge, listen, marched, near, none, quiet, ready, really, stormed, surprise, talking, work

Useful long vowel phonemes
'ai': *again, baby, gave, lane, made, names, page, place, they, today, waited, way*
'ee': *eat, indeed, keep, me, needs, peered, really, see, seen, she, sweet, tea, three, we*
'ie': *lights, myself, night, quiet, right, smiled, time, why, write*

PCM 1 (p.40) reading and spelling *-ed* words
★ Talk about the different pronunciations of *-ed* that are shown on the sheet.
★ Read the words aloud to the children while they listen to the pronunciation. They should then do the activity independently.

PCM 2 (p.41) comprehension
★ Read the questions to the children. Ask them to give the answers orally. (They can find the answers in the book, using the page references given.) Then children can complete the activity independently.

Silly spellings

Join the football to the goal with the rhyming word.

Footballs	Goals
would	white
socks	red
light	good
straight	fox
said	mate
laughed	foot
put	meat
thought	craft
feet	bear
care	port

Focus: different spelling, same pronunciation

What is Rob thinking?

Write Rob's thoughts in each thought bubble.

Focus: developing characterisation

Three ways of saying -ed

Read these *-ed* words aloud. Think about how the *-ed* is said.
Sort the words by writing each one on the hat that has words
with the same *-ed* sound.

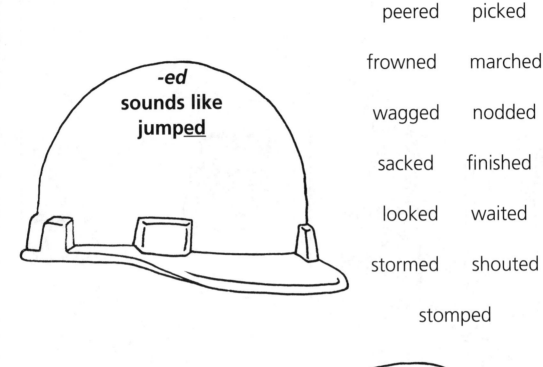

peered	picked
frowned	marched
wagged	nodded
sacked	finished
looked	waited
stormed	shouted
stomped	

**-ed
sounds like
jump<u>ed</u>**

**-ed
sounds like
pull<u>ed</u>**

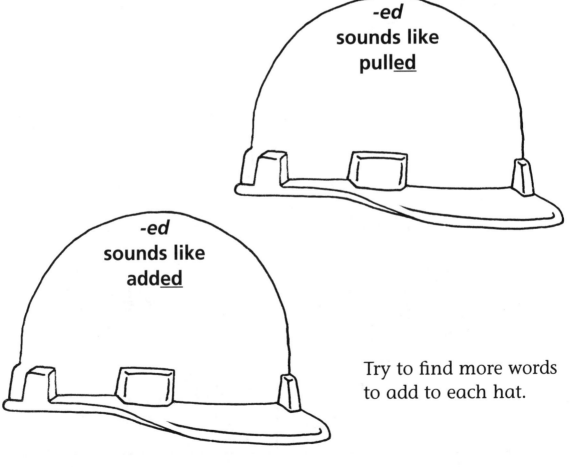

**-ed
sounds like
add<u>ed</u>**

Try to find more words
to add to each hat.

Focus: reading and spelling *-ed* words

What are the answers?

Read the questions.
Write the answers in sentences.

1. What were Sid, Kitty and Amit drinking? (page 3)

_____

2. Who is the boss? (page 3)

_____

3. When must the work at 4 Blue Bog Lane be finished? (page 4)

_____

4. Who is Betty? (page 6)

_____

5. What were Sid, Kitty and Amit eating in the van? (page 10)

_____

6. Why did Betty need the house? (page 13)

_____

7. Where were Sid, Kitty and Amit sitting to do their crossword?
   (page 16)

_____

8. What happened at the end of the story?

_____

_____

_____

Focus: comprehension

Trackers Variety Fiction level 6: Zebra tracks

Author: Robert Swindells
Illustrator: Tony Morris

The Hole

Gaz's story about why a hole suddenly appeared in the middle of his footie pitch.

Total number of words: 779   Number of different words: 312

10 useful high frequency words
across, any, counted, every, ground, still, take, team, way, would

'Tricky' words
attention, cancelled, century, coalmine, collapse, decides, duty, echoey, except, field, flooded, horrible, horror, lightning, lurking, middle, mineshaft, nearly, nineteenth, pitch, swamp, talking, terror, towards, water, winding, worry

Useful long vowel phonemes
'oa': *close, coalmine, holding, hole, know, nobody, notice, over, Rose, soaked*
'ow': *about, bounds, count, down, found, ground, now, out, sounds, wow*
'ee': *creeping, deep, field, keep, leaps, means, nineteenth, really, tea, team, three, we, weeping*

PCM 1 (p.43) writing verbs in the past tense
* ★ Check that children understand the concept of 'past tense'.
* ★ Read the text aloud with the children. Complete some of the work together.

PCM 2 (p.44) using inference
* ★ Discuss what all the characters in the picture are thinking at this point in the story. Ask children to justify their ideas.

Author: Alan Gibbons
Illustrator: Trevor Parkin

Avalanche

If you were lost in an avalanche, would you know what to do? Find out what the narrator did when it happened to him.

Total number of words: 687   Number of different words: 259

10 useful high frequency words
across, couldn't, cried, difficult, ground, pieces, something, sound, still, through

'Tricky' words
avalanche, climbers, deadly, difficult, earth, gloves, half, moment, mountain, move, pieces, thought, tons, whole, world, worried

Useful long vowel phonemes
'ow': *about, around, down, found, ground, loud, mountain, mouth, out, sound, thousands*
'er': *bursts, earth, first, hurt, turn, were, word, working, world*
'ue': *blue, boom, huge, move, pure, through, too*

PCM 1 (p.45) same spelling, different pronunciation
* ★ Read all the words in each set aloud with the children before they begin the activity.

PCM 2 (p.46) summarising the story
* ★ Complete the activity orally before the children begin to write.

From present to past

Replace the underlined verbs in each sentence with the same verbs in the past tense.

One night there <u>is</u> *was* this wild storm. The rain <u>hits</u> my window and

<u>keeps</u> me awake.

At school, the playing field <u>is</u> like a swamp. But me and my

mates still <u>want</u> a game of footie.

At morning break we <u>go</u> to the field. Miss Rose <u>is</u> on duty.

She <u>says</u>, "That field's like a swamp."

I <u>pick</u> my team, Robbo <u>picks</u>

his. We <u>are</u> about to kick off

when Robbo <u>says</u>, "Hey, look

at this."

I <u>look</u>. In the middle of the

pitch <u>is</u> a hole. I <u>go</u> as close as I

<u>dare</u>.

Focus: writing verbs in the past tense

What are they thinking?

Look carefully at the picture. What are the characters thinking? Draw thought bubbles and write in them what Miss Rose, Gaz and Colin might be thinking.

Focus: using inference

Odd one out

Read all the words in each set aloud.
In each set, the letter pattern is pronounced differently in one of the words. Circle the odd one out each time.

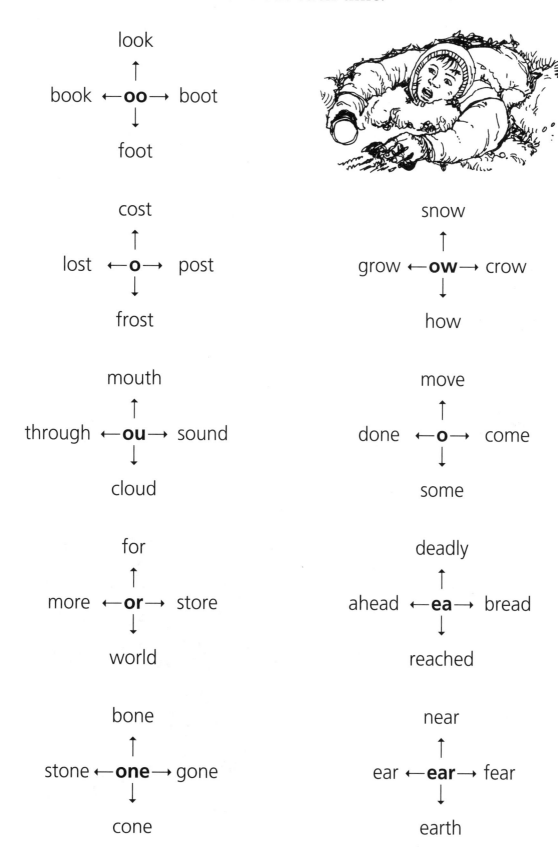

look

↑

book ←**oo**→ boot

↓

foot

cost

↑

lost ←**o**→ post

↓

frost

snow

↑

grow ←**ow**→ crow

↓

how

mouth

↑

through ←**ou**→ sound

↓

cloud

move

↑

done ←**o**→ come

↓

some

for

↑

more ←**or**→ store

↓

world

deadly

↑

ahead ←**ea**→ bread

↓

reached

bone

↑

stone ←**one**→ gone

↓

cone

near

↑

ear ←**ear**→ fear

↓

earth

Focus: same spelling, different pronunciation

45

What did he write?

The boy wrote a summary of what happened for his teacher. He wrote two sentences beside each picture he drew. Write what you think he wrote.

Dad and I went into the mountains. We got lost and it started snowing.

_____

_____

_____

_____

_____

_____

_____

_____

_____

_____

_____

_____

_____

_____

46

Focus: summarising the story

Reading profile for *Bear tracks, Elephant tracks* and *Frog tracks*

Child's name _____   Assessment date _____

Home language _____   Date of birth _____

Reading for meaning

Bear tracks
- re-reads a simple book and retains overall meaning?   YES / NO
- with help, can read simple sentences?   YES / NO
- remembers character names and reads them correctly next time they appear?   YES / NO
- uses some features of a word to 'guess' what the word says, not always accurately?   YES / NO
- uses pictures to identify the main topic?   YES / NO
- can talk about pictures and attempt to find new information in the writing?   YES / NO

Elephant tracks
- expects the text to make sense?   YES / NO
- predicts a word using syntactic cues?   YES / NO
- predicts a word using picture cues?   YES / NO
- has a sense of 'what has been read so far'?   YES / NO
- expresses opinions about the text?   YES / NO
- predicts contents of a book using the cover?   YES / NO
- uses pictures for information?   YES / NO

Frog tracks
- is aware of an unrecognised word and hesitates?   YES / NO
- is aware when meaning has been lost?   YES / NO
- re-reads familiar text independently?   YES / NO
- uses pictures to add detail and gain meaning?   YES / NO

Phonic skills

Bear tracks
- accurate, consistent recognition of all letter sounds?   YES / NO
- can identify words that 'begin with' each of the common sounds?   YES / NO
- hears all three sounds in a CVC word?   YES / NO
- knows that initial letter sound can be used to predict a word?   YES / NO

Elephant tracks
- reads and writes CVC words?   YES / NO
- uses phonic knowledge to recognise initial letter of a word?   YES / NO
- makes accurate and consistent use of letter sounds to confirm words?   YES / NO

Frog tracks
- consistently reads initial consonant blends?   YES / NO
- consistently reads final consonant blends?   YES / NO
- blends consonants and short vowel phonemes together to decode words?   YES / NO
- recognises common word endings (*-ing*, *-ed*, etc.)   YES / NO

Reading profile for *Giraffe tracks, Parrot tracks, Tiger tracks* and *Zebra tracks*

Child's name _____   Assessment date _____

Home language _____   Date of birth _____

Reading for meaning

Giraffe tracks
- reads familiar text aloud with fluency?   YES / NO
- attempts to self-correct?   YES / NO
- uses syntax and semantics to try to recover meaning?   YES / NO
- uses text to make accurate predictions?   YES / NO
- answers 'information retrieval' questions?   YES / NO

Parrot tracks
- is fluent when reading unfamiliar text aloud?   YES / NO
- begins to read with expression?   YES / NO
- uses punctuation to guide intonation?   YES / NO
- begins to use some simple inference?   YES / NO
- locates specific information in the text?   YES / NO

Tiger tracks
- reads ahead to make sense of the text?   YES / NO
- reads simple text with accuracy and expression?   YES / NO
- discusses how a character may act?   YES / NO
- discusses why an event occurred?   YES / NO
- can use inference to answer questions?   YES / NO

Zebra tracks
- uses contextual knowledge to find words that 'fit'?   YES / NO
- can read silently, perhaps mouthing words?   YES / NO
- can find evidence in a text to answer questions about character or action?   YES / NO
- discusses what a character might do or say?   YES / NO
- is sensitive to author's language use?   YES / NO

Phonic skills

Giraffe tracks
- recognises common long vowel phonemes?   YES / NO
- blends consonants and long vowel phonemes together?   YES / NO
- identifies words that rhyme?   YES / NO
- recognises a significant number of familiar high frequency words in running text?   YES / NO

Parrot tracks
- recognises less common long vowel phonemes?   YES / NO
- segments a two-syllable word into syllables?   YES / NO
- with help, recognises familiar 'chunks' of words and uses this to decode new words?   YES / NO

Tiger tracks
- segments a polysyllabic word into syllables?   YES / NO
- recognises familiar 'chunks' of a word and uses this to decode new words?   YES / NO
- knows that words that look similar can sound different?   YES / NO

Zebra tracks
- recognises letter patterns representing common word endings, e.g. *-tion*?   YES / NO
- recognises common suffixes and prefixes?   YES / NO